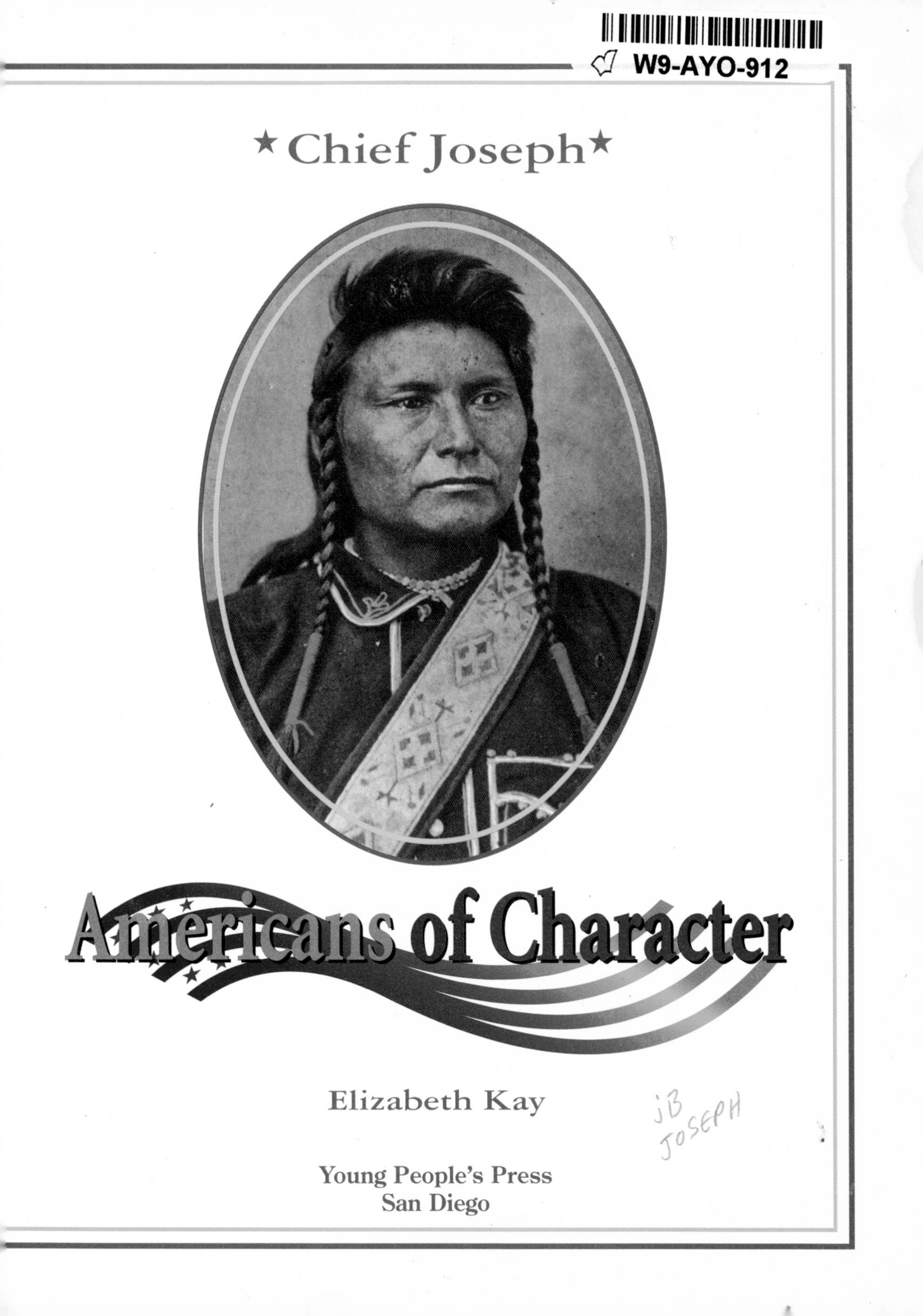

★Chief Joseph★

Americans of Character

Elizabeth Kay

Young People's Press
San Diego

About the *"Six Pillars of Character"*

Each section of this book includes a drawing of a pillar. Above each pillar is a word. These words—six in all—name the most important traits that a person of good character has. Together, these words are known as the *"Six Pillars of Character."* On pages 22 – 27 you will be exploring what these pillars mean.

Requests for permission to make copies of any part of the work should be mailed to: Permissions, Young People's Press, Inc. 1731 Kettner Blvd., San Diego, California 92101.

Cover, UPI/Corbis-Bettmann.

Published in the United States of America.

1 2 3 4 5 6 7 8 9 - 02 01 00 99 98 97

ISBN 1-57279-062-8

Table of Contents

INTRODUCTION

The story of Chief Joseph is the story of his people, the Nez Perce. He lived in a time of great change for Native Americans. Strangers were moving onto their land—strangers who had very different ideas. How could the different groups share the land? Many talks and fights were about this question.

In the end, the settlers forced the Nez Perce off their land, the land they had lived on for thousands of years. But Chief Joseph never quit trying to help his people get home. With great dignity he led the Nez Perce and fought for their rights.

Chief Joseph was an American of character.

CITIZENSHIP

1ST TREATY

A treaty is an agreement written down on a piece of paper. Native Americans and the U.S. government wrote many treaties to try to solve problems they faced.

The first treaty between the Nez Perce and the U.S. government was signed by Joseph's father, Tuekakas, in 1855.

Joseph was 15 years old. The treaty was called the Walla Walla Treaty. It said the Nez Perce would share some of their land with the settlers. By the time Tuekakas died in 1871, however, Joseph knew that the settlers did not want to share the land. They wanted the Indians *off* the land!

Joseph had promised his father he would never sell the Nez Perce land. He never did, even though trying to keep the land became a terrible hardship.

The Walla Walla Council, 1855

2 SONS

Old Joseph, Tuekakas, had two sons. Young Joseph, whose Indian name means "thunder rolling in the mountains," was born first, in 1840. A few years later, another son was born. His name, Ollokot, means "frog." The two brothers looked alike but acted very differently. Young Joseph was thoughtful and quiet. Ollokot did everything fast, from riding to fighting.

Young Joseph grew up to be a great, thoughtful leader of his people. Ollokot grew up to be a brave warrior who gave his life defending the Nez Perce.

As Chief, Joseph always thought before he acted. Even people who would come to be his enemies saw his greatness. U.S. Colonel Nelson Miles, the person to whom Chief Joseph eventually had to surrender, described Joseph as very wise.

Chief Joseph thought carefully before making decisions.

RESPONSIBILITY

3 BILLION ACRES

It is estimated that Native Americans once roamed 3 billion acres of land that are now the United States of America. The earth was sacred to them, much too sacred to be owned or bought or sold. Land was like a Mother to them; the sky housed The Great Father; and animals and plants were Brothers and Sisters. In this way, Native Americans were one with nature.

Chief Joseph shared these beliefs. As he said, **"The earth was created by the assistance of the sun, and it should be left as it was. . . The country was made without lines. . . and it is no man's business to divide it up."** Chief Joseph wanted the land for his people, but he also wanted the land to be left unspoiled.

CITIZENSHIP

Chief Joseph believed in protecting the environment.

4-MONTH RACE FOR FREEDOM

Chief Joseph tried to do the right thing. He talked over problems without fighting. He tried to protect his people and to get along with the U.S. Army.

Years passed and promises were broken. Finally, in 1877, the Nez Perce agreed to go live on a reservation. It would mean giving up their freedom to roam, but it would be better than war. Chief Joseph led his tribe as they said good-bye to their beloved land. They gathered on a prairie for a final taste of freedom.

Then things went wrong. A group of young Nez Perce warriors, unhappy with the decision, attacked some white settlements. The Nez Perce

CARING

found themselves being chased by the Army. For four months, they raced for Canada—for freedom—through mountains, valleys, snow, and rain. Chief Joseph, afraid for the women, children, and elderly, wanted desperately to avoid any more fights: **“We intended to go peaceably to the buffalo country and leave the question of returning to our country to be settled afterward.”**

Chief Joseph cared most about his people’s safety.

5TH DAY OF OCTOBER

On October 5, 1877, the Nez Perce's four-month ordeal ended. The leader of the Army, Colonel Miles, promised to return the Nez Perce to the Northwest. Chief Joseph believed him. He wanted the fighting to end. Only 87 men, 184 women, and 147 children were left.

From his camp in the Bear Paw Mountains of Montana, Chief Joseph rode out to meet the Army. Five warriors walked beside him. He surrendered with these famous words: **"It is cold and we have no blankets. The children are freezing to death. . . Hear me, my chiefs. I am tired; my heart is sick and sad. From where the sun now stands, I will fight no more forever."**

RESPONSIBILITY

When the consequences of fighting for his people became too great, Chief Joseph surrendered.

6-ty Miles Away

When Chief Joseph surrendered, the Nez Perce were less than 60 miles from Canada. One more day's march was all they needed to reach freedom. But the U.S. Army had them surrounded. They would not let the Nez Perce go peacefully.

Chief Joseph had tried his very best to get his people to freedom. He would never stop trying to get them home.

Chief Joseph kept trying to do what was best for his people.

RESPECT FOR OTHERS

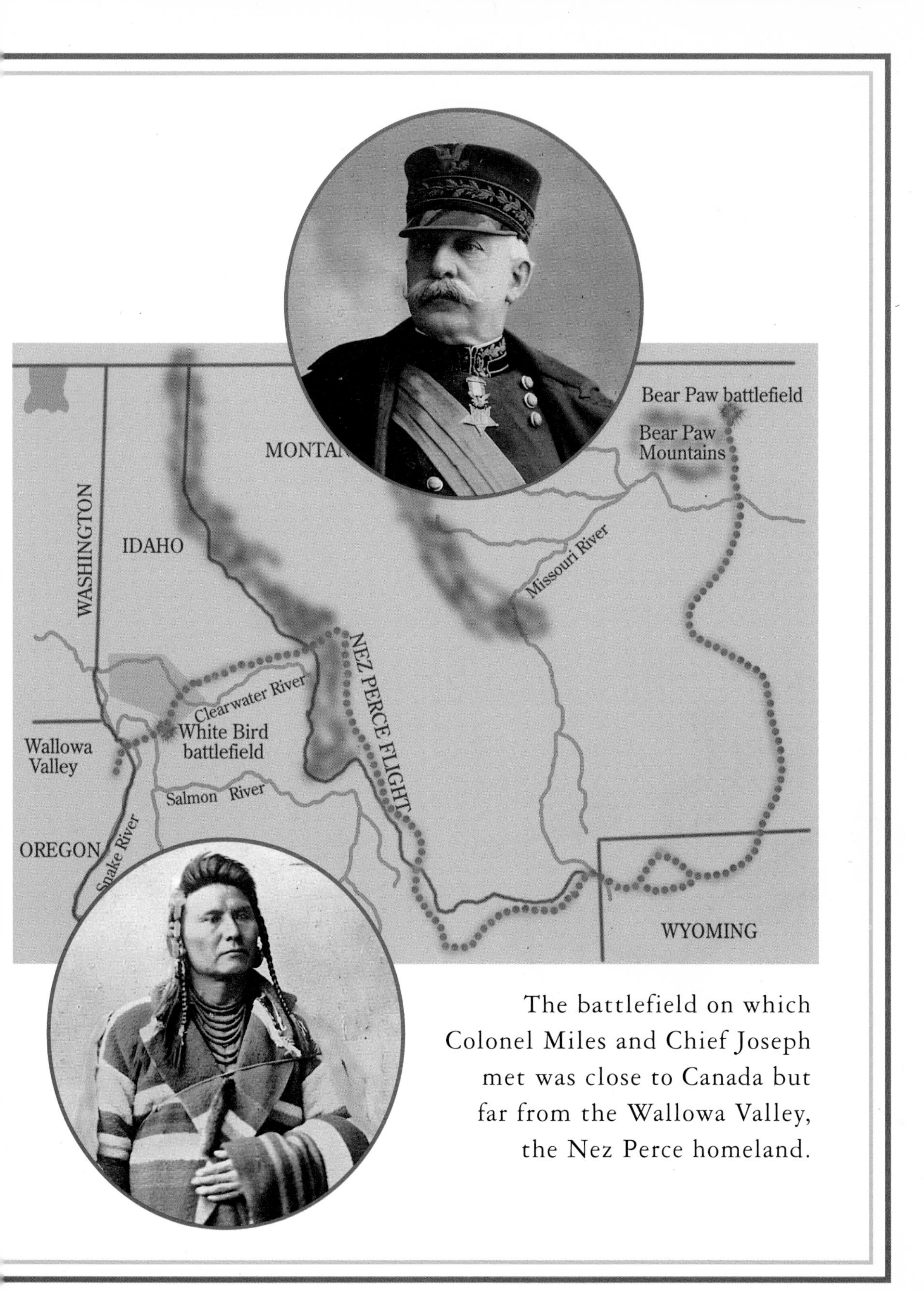

The battlefield on which Colonel Miles and Chief Joseph met was close to Canada but far from the Wallowa Valley, the Nez Perce homeland.

7 Letters in Wallowa

The beautiful area in which the Nez Perce had lived for thousands of years is known as the Wallowa Valley. There they had winter homes in the valley and summer camps on the plateaus. The land was rich, with plenty of food to hunt, fish, and gather.

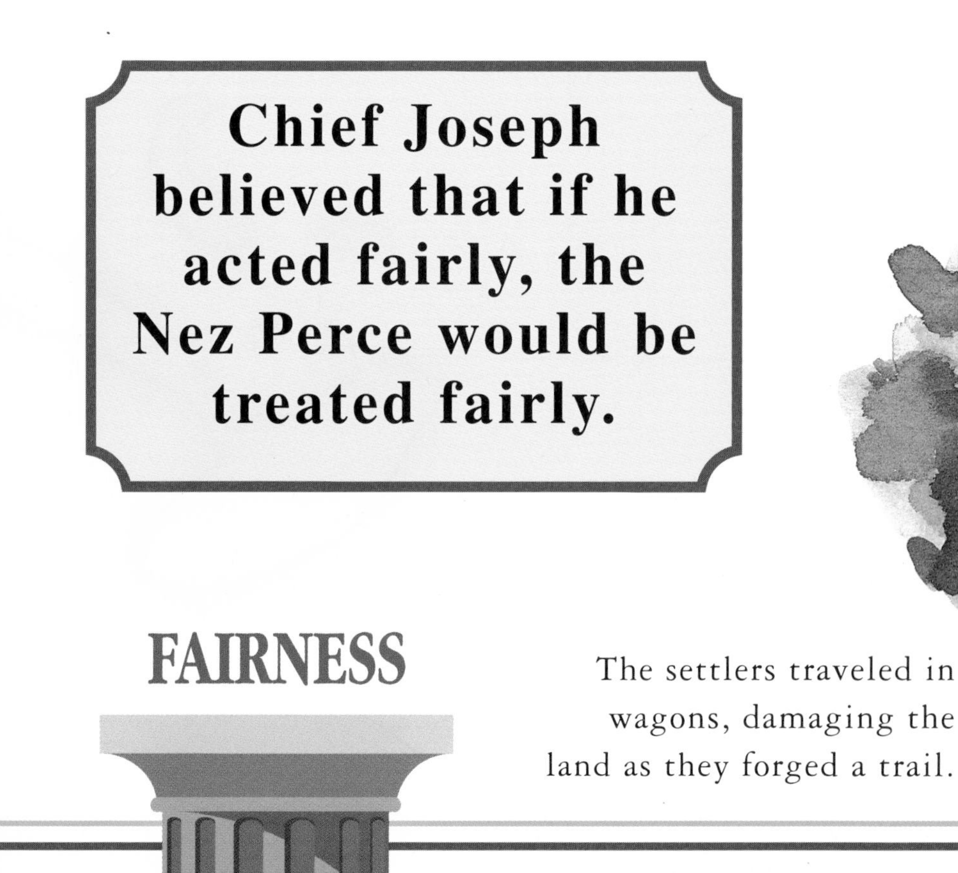

The settlers traveled in wagons, damaging the land as they forged a trail.

The famous Oregon Trail went through the Wallowa Valley. That's how settlers and explorers first began entering the Nez Perce land. They loved it for different reasons—for the furs and gold they found there and the money these things could bring them.

Chief Joseph never stopped loving the Wallowa. As he said, **"It may never again be our home, but my father sleeps there, and I love it as I love my mother. I left there hoping to avoid bloodshed."**

8 Years in Exile

When Chief Joseph surrendered, he believed the Nez Perce would be allowed to return to their homeland. Instead, they were taken as prisoners to Kansas. They stayed there for eight months before being exiled to Indian Territory for eight years. The Nez Perce called the land in Kansas and Oklahoma *Eekish-Pah*, "The Hot Place."

During these years of exile, Chief Joseph often told the sad story of the Nez Perce. Always he spoke with dignity. More and more people listened to him. Finally, in 1885, the Nez Perce were moved back to the Northwest—but to Washington and Idaho, not the Wallowa Valley.

In 1904, Chief Joseph died on the Colville Reservation in Washington. He had never been allowed to live again in his beloved home.

TRUSTWORTHINESS

Chief Joseph stood up for his beliefs.

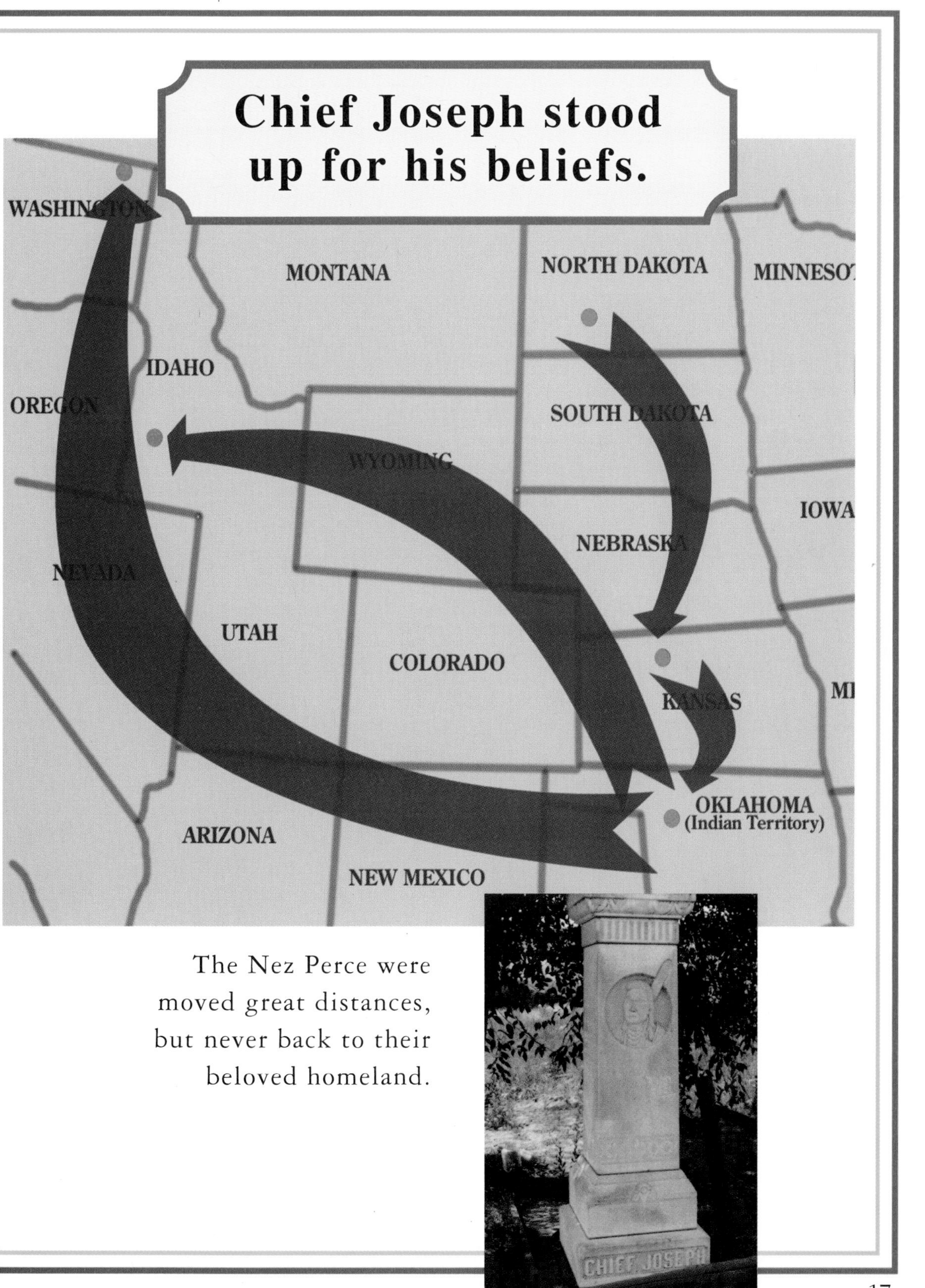

The Nez Perce were moved great distances, but never back to their beloved homeland.

9-ty Miles from Home

To this day, the Nez Perce have not been allowed to reclaim their homeland in the Wallowa Valley. Their closest settlement, the Nez Perce Reservation in Idaho, is some 90 miles away by car. Farther away still is the Colville Reservation where Chief Joseph died.

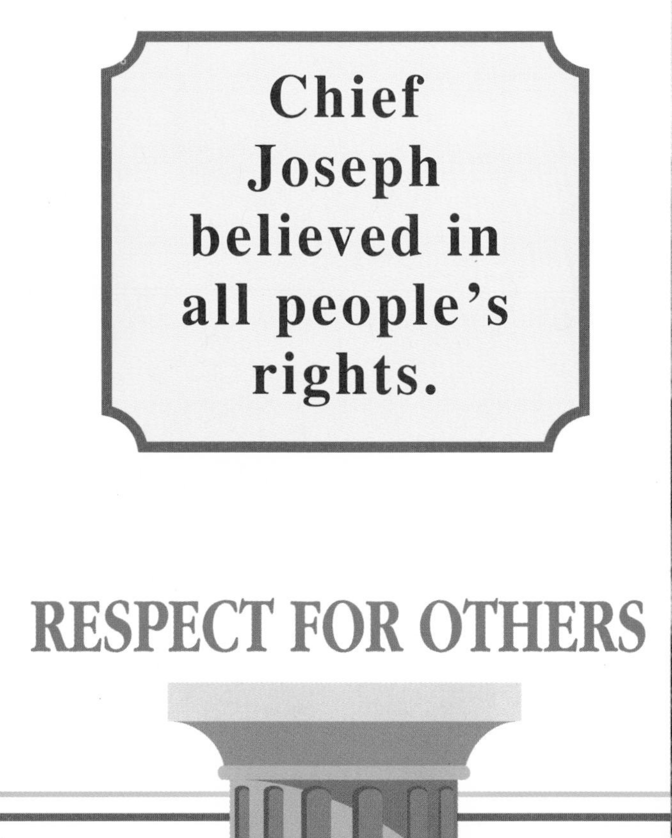

Some say Chief Joseph died of a broken heart. But the dignity with which he represented his people makes this unlikely. He stood quietly and firmly for his beliefs until the end. Perhaps most of all, Chief Joseph believed in peace. As he said, **"If the white man wants to live in peace with the Indian he can live in peace. There need be no trouble. Treat all men alike. Give them all an equal chance to live and grow."**

These photos were taken recently on the Nez Perce Reservation in Idaho.

10 Letters in Prospector

In 1860, prospectors discovered gold in the Nez Perce territory. From that time on, it became harder and harder to keep the settlers from taking over the Wallowa Valley. Greedy gold miners completely ignored the Walla Walla Treaty in their love of money. Future treaties were equally meaningless. With sadness, Chief Joseph would ask:

Chief Joseph wanted to protect natural resources for future generations.

"When will the white man learn to tell the truth?" With even more sadness he would watch the prospectors tear up the beautiful land, wasting the resources Mother Earth provided. He knew the Nez Perce way of life was lost forever.

CITIZENSHIP

The "*Six Pillars of Character*"

Look for the Trustworthiness pillar on the pages about Chief Joseph. Write what you think trustworthiness means. Some ideas are given below.

Look for the Respect for Others pillar on the pages about Chief Joseph. Write what you think respect for others means. Some ideas are given below.

RESPECT FOR OTHERS

Be courteous and polite.

Respect the right of people to make decisions about their own lives.

Appreciate and accept differences.

Look for the Responsibility pillar on the pages about Chief Joseph. Write what you think responsibility means. Some ideas are given below.

Look for the Fairness pillar on the pages about Chief Joseph. Write what you think fairness means. Some ideas are given below.

Look for the Caring pillar on the pages about Chief Joseph. Write what you think caring means. Some ideas are given below.

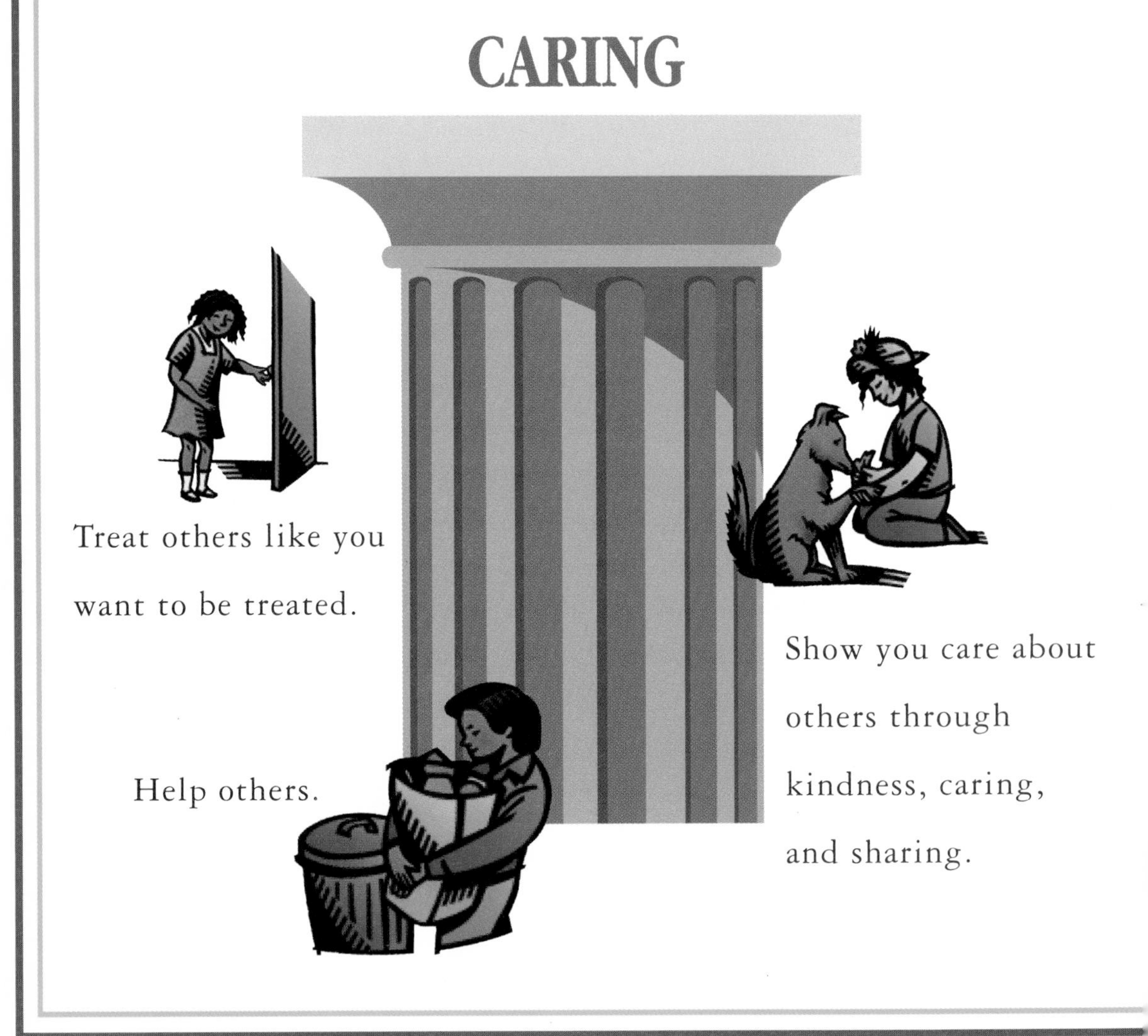

Look for the Citizenship pillar on the pages about Chief Joseph. Write what you think citizenship means. Some ideas are given below.

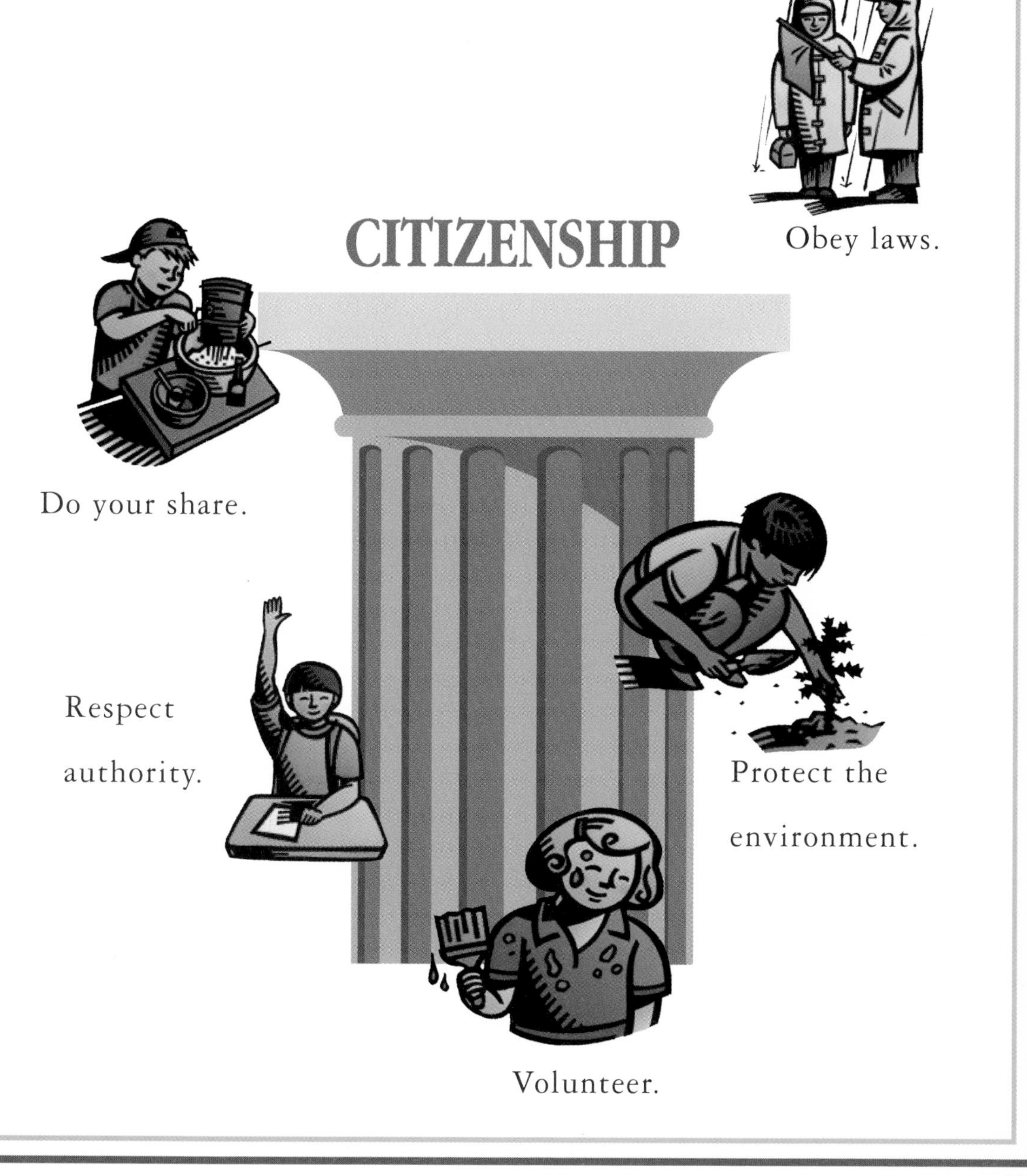

Acknowledgments

The author expresses her special thanks to her daughter, Margaret Kinkead, for being proud of her work.

The publisher gratefully acknowledges permission to use the following photographs:

Page i, UPI/Corbis-Bettmann; iv, 21, The Bettmann Archive; 2-3, Washington State Historical Society (Tacoma, WA); 7, © Telegraph Colour Library/FPG; iii, 8-9, Special Collections Division, University of Washington Libraries, Negative No. N.A. #947; 12 (top and bottom), Montana Historical Society, Helena; 17, United States Department of the Interior, National Park Service, Nez Perce National Historical Park; 18-19 (both), Courtesy of Jerry Todd/ Nez Perce Tribe; 20, Corbis-Bettmann.

Illustrations pages ii, 5, 11, 15, 28 by John Edens/Creative Freelancers.
Illustrations pages 22-27 by Tracy Sabin.